CW00867002

THE HOLY SPIRIT PROPHETIC POETIC JOURNAL

REV. DR. SANNETH BROWN

Reaching the World with a Supernatural Prophetic Word

WESTBOW
PRESS®
A DIVISION OF THOMAS NELSON
& ZONDERVAN

Scripture taken from the King James Version of the Bible.

WestBow Press books may be ordered through booksellers or by contacting:

WestBow Press
A Division of Thomas Nelson & Zondervan
1663 Liberty Drive
Bloomington, IN 47403
www.westbowpress.com
1 (866) 928-1240

ISBN: 978-1-9736-5894-8 (sc)
ISBN: 978-1-9736-5895-5 (hc)
ISBN: 978-1-9736-5917-4 (e)

Library of Congress Control Number: 2019904073

Print information available on the last page.

WestBow Press rev. date: 4/22/2019

(Eph. 3:14–21)

For this cause I bow my knees unto the Father of our Lord Jesus
Christ, Of whom the whole family in heaven and earth is named,
That he would grant you, according to the riches of his glory, to
be strengthened with might by his Spirit in the inner man; That
Christ may dwell in your hearts by faith; that ye, being rooted
and grounded in love, May be able to comprehend with all saints
what is the breadth, and length, and depth, and height; And to
know the love of Christ, which passeth knowledge, that ye might
be filled with all the fulness of God. Now unto him that is able to
do exceeding abundantly above all that we ask or think, according
to the power that worketh in us, Unto him be glory in the church
by Christ Jesus throughout all ages, world without end. Amen.

Introduction

This prodigious Holy Spirit–filled inspiring journal is a blend of scriptures, quotes, and prophetic thoughts that are designed to keep your focus on the inherent, revealed, impressive, and infallible word of the Almighty God. This will help you to develop a greater love for the word of God and experience intimacy.

The Holy Spirit Prophetic Poetic Journal is also designed to:

- uplift your spirit to dimensions that you have never been to before in Jesus Christ,
- strengthen your mind and keep your mind in perfect peace, and
- ignite your soul so that you will continue your upward climb, increase your faith, and achieve all that God destined for you!

This journal is inviting and will have you mediate, reflect, and discover your worth in God.

"He hath made every thing beautiful in his time: also he hath set the world in their heart, so that no man can find out the work that God maketh from the beginning to the end." (Ecc. 3:11)

"For the earnest expectation of the creature waiteth for the manifestation of the sons of God" (Rom. 8:19)

I am a sign, a wonder, and a miracle. I am recognized in heaven as God's end-time Holy Ghost trooper, and I am feared in hell and by the powers of darkness!

I will hold my head high. My hard work, faith, commitment, perseverance, and endurance over this lifetime have brought me here today, to write this The Holy Spirit Prophetic Poetic Journal. I will arise and shine now for my light has come and the glory of the Lord is risen upon me. I can distinctively see God's revealed, radiant light at the end of my tunnel. And although my journey is far from over, I have come this far by the grace of Almighty God! The time has come for God to favor me. The time has come to walk into my destiny and fulfill all that God has in store for me. This time has come, and now is the time of great acceleration, double anointing, double dreams, double visions, double revelation, and the thousand-times blessings from the God of my salvation. It is my time to manifest my highest will. It is my time of truly stepping into my divine path with confidence in what I am on earth to do, and God will guide me on how to do it. It is a time of hope, dreams, visions, and revelations to manifest. The true greatness of who I am is ready to express itself fully! Isaiah 60:1 says, "Arise, shine; for thy light is come, and the glory of the LORD is risen upon thee."

My life has moved from one of oppression, denial, and poverty to one of a victorious warrior, powerful remnant, and a Holy Ghost–filled champion. What I have endured in my past I will use as fuel for my extraordinary future. John 21:25 reads, "And there are also many other things which Jesus did, the which, if they should be written every one, I suppose that even the world itself could not contain the books that should be written. Amen." I would not be able to write a book containing all the things that I have been through in my life from birth until now. However, I have confidence in saying that everything that I have been through in my life is not just my testimony but is my collected history. My enormous testimony is that Yahweh Ropheka healed, restored, renewed, and reenergized me and set me free, never again to be in bondage and fear! I now declare boldly that I am saved, sanctified, Holy Ghost filled, and water and fire baptized in the name of God the Father, Son, and Holy Ghost! I am called, I am chosen, I am anointed, I am appointed, and now I am ready to enter into my destiny because he that began a good work in me is able to complete it successfully. I am persuaded that God is about to do phenomenal supernatural things in my life. It is my time to achieve angelic, adventurous, exceptional accomplishments and to accept my heavenly Father's greatness. God will do exceedingly and above all that I can ask or imagine.

> "And being fully persuaded that, what he had promised, he was able also to perform." (Rom. 4:21)

"And God is able to make all grace abound toward you; that ye, always having all sufficiency in all things, may abound to every good work:" (2 Cor. 9:8)

"I shall not die, but live, and declare the works of the LORD." (Ps. 118:17)

"I am as a wonder unto many; but thou art my strong refuge." (Ps. 71:7)

I am an atmosphere changer and am anointed for God's service. Through the power of the Holy Ghost, I am swifter than eagles! God wrote my life, and that is poetic.

These characteristics best describe me.

I am God's beautiful one-of-a-kind masterpiece!
I am God's outstanding work! I am optimistic! I am spiritual! I am passionate!
I am prosperous! I am swift! I am truthful!
I am qualified! I am valuable! I am profound!
I am unique! I am vibrant! I am remarkable! I am elegant!
I am vivacious! I am resourceful! I am successful!
I am gifted and talented! I am thankful! I am radiant!
I am resolute! I am tenacious! I am vigorous! I am thriving!
I am superb! I am timely! I am terrific! I am splendid!
I am skillful! I am sensible! I am serene!
I am sharing! I am caring! I am loving! I am respected!
I am secure! I am rewarding! I am robust!
I am reasonable! I am reliable! I am content!
I am persevering! I am playful! I am inventive!
I am productive! I am precious! I am joyous!
I am kind! I am limitless! I am luminous! I am innovative!

Problems + Situations + Circumstances = The Bible

The Bible is all in one and has all the answers to life's many problems, situations, and circumstances.

- For hope, read 1 Corinthians 15:54–58 and John 3:16.
- For depression, read Psalm 40:1–3 and 1 Peter 5:6–7.
- For future plans, read Jeremiah 29:11.
- For beauty, read Isaiah 61:2–3.
- For loneliness, read Isaiah 41:10, Psalm 23:4, Hebrews 13:1–25, and Genesis 2:18.
- For marital problems, read James 5:16, 1 Corinthians 7:2–5, Proverbs 10:12, Ephesians 5:25, Proverbs 5:15–19, Matthew 19:5–6, 1 Corinthians 7:1–16, Ephesians 5:21–33, Colossians 3:18–19, 1 Peter 3:1–7, and Hebrews 13:4.
- For problems with children, read Deuteronomy 6:1–25, Ephesians 6:4, Matthew 6:33, and Proverbs 22:6.
- For suicidal thoughts and tendencies, read 1 John 1:9, Exodus 20:13, Revelation 21:8, 2 Corinthians 11:14, 1 Corinthians 10:13, and John 8:44.
- If you are fearful, read Revelation 21:8, Matthew 14:27, Revelation 20:6, Acts 4:12, and Genesis 3:4.
- If you are doubtful, read Proverbs 3:5–8, James 1:6, Matthew 21:21, and Jude 1:22.
- If you are addicted to cigarettes, drugs, or alcohol, read 1 Peter 5:8, Titus 2:1–8, Romans 13:13–14, Ephesians 5:18, 2 Timothy 4:5, and Proverbs 20:1.
- If you are struggling with sexual immorality, such as pornography, read 1 Corinthians 7:3–5, Hebrews 13:4, Genesis 2:24, Proverbs 18–19, Matthew 5:28, and Genesis 39:7–10.

- If you are a liar, read Proverbs 19:9, John 8:44, Proverbs 14:5, Proverbs 26:23–28, 1 John 1:9, and Romans 3:13.
- If you have school problems, read Philippians 4:13, 1 Timothy 4:12, 1 Corinthians 10:31, Proverbs 2:6, Proverbs 13:20, and 2 Timothy 2:15.
- If you need a good friend, read Proverbs 18:24, John 15:13, Proverbs 17:17, Proverbs 27:9, John 15:12, James 2:23, Matthew 18:15, and Proverbs 22:11.
- If you are a bully, read Matthew 25:40, Isaiah 29:20, John 12:48, Mark 10:14, Jude 1:4, Joshua 1:9, Psalm 10:7–9, and Isaiah 59:7.
- If you want to know God, read Isaiah 40:28, Revelation 1:8, Jeremiah 10:10, Jeremiah 51:15, Psalm 147:5, James 1:17, Psalm 33:4, Proverbs 16:7, Acts 17:24–26, John 3:16, Psalm 97:2, Jeremiah 12:1, Isaiah 48:17, Isaiah 41:4, Psalm 104:24, Psalm 100:5, and Psalm 33:5.
- For healing, read Isaiah 41:10, Jeremiah 33:6, 1 Peter 2:24, Isaiah 53:5, Psalm 103:2–4, James 5:15, 3 John 1:2, Matthew 10:1, and Proverbs 17:22.
- If you need restoration, read Joel 2:25–26, Jeremiah 30:17, Psalm 51:12, Isaiah 61:7, Acts 3:19–21, Revelation 21:1–5, 1 Peter 5:10, Zachariah 9:12, and Mark 11:24.
- If you need deliverance, read Psalm 34:17, Psalm 107:6, 2 Samuel 22:2, Psalm 50:15, James 5:16, Galatians 5:1, Psalm 40:13, Romans 12:1–2, Matthew 10:1, and Isaiah 43:1–5.
- If your need prosperity, read Deuteronomy 8:18, Jeremiah 29:11, Philippians 4:19, Malachi 3:19, 3 John 1:2, Psalm 128:2, Joshua 1:9, Proverbs 28:25, Job 22:23–27, and Zechariah 9:12.
- For wealth, read Hebrews 13:5, 1 Timothy 6:10, Matthew 6:19–21, Matthew 6:24, Luke 12:33–34, Acts 2:44–45, Malachi 3:10–12, Acts 2:32–35, Proverbs 13:22, Deuteronomy 8:18, Proverbs 28:22, Luke 16:11, and Ephesians 4:28.
- For divine health, read Proverbs 17:22, 1 Corinthians 3:17, Proverbs 16:24, 1 Corinthians 10:31, 1 Timothy 4:7–8, 1 John 4:18, 1 Corinthians 3:16, 1 Peter 2:25, 1 John 4:18, Leviticus 19:28, and John 10:10.
- For wisdom, read James 1:5, James 3:17, Proverbs 3:13–18, Ephesians 5:15–17, Proverbs 10:23, Colossians 3:16, Job 12:12–13, Luke 21:15, 2 Timothy 2:7, Proverbs 17:10, and Proverbs 1:7.

- For knowledge, read Proverbs 18:15, Proverbs 2:10, Proverbs 1:7, Hosea 4:6–7, Proverbs 24:5, Proverbs 8:10, Genesis 3:22, Proverbs 2:10–11, James 3:13–18, and James 2:1–10.
- For understanding, read 2 Thessalonians 5:21, John 3:16, Micah 5:2, 1 John 5:13, 1 Corinthians 13:1–13, Romans 6:1–23, Acts 2:1–47, John 14:26, John 14:6, Isaiah 1:1–31, and Matthew 1:1–25.
- To worship God, read Exodus 20:4–5, Psalm 150, Matthew 4:10, Mark 7:7, John 4:23–24, and Romans 12:1.
- To fast, read Leviticus 16:29 and 23:32, Ezra 10:6, Isaiah 58:6, Matthew 6:16–18 and 17:21, and Acts 13:2–3.
- To fight temptation, read Psalm 95:8, Luke 22:40, 1 Corinthians 10:13, James 1:2–12:2, and Peter 2:9.
- For parenting, read Deuteronomy 6:5–7, Proverbs 13:24 and 19:18; Colossians 3:20–21, and Ephesians 6:4.
- For work, read Ecclesiastes 5:18–20, Colossians 3:23, and 1 Thessalonians 3:7–14.
- For patience, read Psalm 37:7–9, Galatians 5:22, Colossians 1:11, 1 Thessalonians 5:14, Hebrews 12:1, and James 1:3–4.
- For hurt from others, read Matthew 6:12–15, Mark 11:25, Colossians 3:12–15, Romans 12:9–19.
- To love one another, read Matthew 5:43–48, John 15:9–13, and 1 Corinthians 13.

(Luke 4:18–19)

"The Spirit of the Lord is upon me, because he hath anointed me to preach the gospel to the poor; he hath sent me to heal the brokenhearted, to preach deliverance to the captives, and recovering of sight to the blind, to set at liberty them that are bruised, To preach the acceptable year of the Lord."

The Spirit of the Lord is upon me to do great exploits in this generation!

The Holy Spirit is my ignition.

(Joel 2:28)

I will prophesy with the power of the Holy
Spirit with accuracy and precision.

The spirit of the Lord will manifest upon all flesh.

(Psalm 139:14)

I am my creator's masterpiece, and I am original.

I was created by my creator's love, and his
promises were embalmed within me.

(Ephesians 4:6)

God is one in three persons—blessed trinity.

God the Father, Son, and Holy Ghost is wrapped up in the Trinity.

(1 Peter 2:9-10)

I am my heavenly Father's treasured gift.

My relationship with my heavenly Father is divine.

(Romans 10:10)

When I confess Jesus Christ, I am blessed.

My mouth will speak of God in the east, west, north, and south.

(John 10:10)

Joy is now, so enjoy and let no one annoy.

I will enjoy the abundant life with free will and fulfill.

(Mark 8:8)

I am full and running over with God's goodness.

Seven baskets left; that's God's providential provision.

(Ephesians 3:3–4)

The revelation of Christ is the Holy Ghost revealed.

The wisdom, knowledge, and understanding
of Christ is Holy Spirit revealed.

(Acts 1:8)

The Holy Spirit's anointing will rain on the earth.

The power of the Holy Ghost is the evidence
of Jesus Christ arisen from death.

(Isaiah 60:1–3)

I will rise, shine, and align in Christ.

God's cloud of glory is all over me.

(Isaiah 61:3)

I am anointed with joy and hope to cope.

I am appointed to express God's exuberant praise.

(Isaiah 40:8)

The word of God will neither wither nor fade.

God's word is food and water to my thirsty soul.

(2 Corinthians 5:17)

I am a new creature in Christ and his preacher.

Christ died for me and gave me breakthroughs.

(Ps. 145:3)

God's greatness is blameless and with brightness.

God's greatness would take me all of eternity to search out.

(Psalm 103:1–5)

I confess that I will not be depressed because I am healed.

Wherever I go I will gain the spirit's access to possess.

(John 3:16-17)

Jesus Christ's DNA was love for humanity.

Jesus Christ died for all nations because he
loves all the nations of the earth.

(Ezekiel 33:4–7)

Prophets and prophetesses are God's voice on earth.

Prophets and prophetesses are foreordained to declare and decree God's words with accuracy and precision.

(John 4:13–14)

Jesus Christ is water that, once you drink, you never thirst again.

Jesus Christ's water gives complete satisfaction and contentment.

(Job 42:12–13)

The blessings of the Lord will be given on gold platters.

The farmer's trials may be hotter, but it is the latter blessings that matter.

(Psalm 1:3)

The righteous fruits will show Christ's attributes.

The righteous bear all seasons' fruits.

(Psalm 2:8)

My inheritance from God is evidence of goodness.

Jesus Christ is my possession so I will move forward in progression.
God's inheritance is a possibility and not an impossibility.

(John 11:35)

Jesus wept.
Jesus wept, and my tithes and offerings he accepts.

Jesus wept, and his tears are emblems of love.

John 11:25–27

In Christ my sins are forgiven, and now I am alive.

By the Holy Ghost's power, I am revived.

(Matthew 13:3–9)

My faith will increase by hearing the word of God.

My ear will hear the words of the Lord, and I shall live.

(Matthew 10:6–10)

Christ's divine healing is always in season.

Jesus Christ's blood breaks through any barrier.

Matthew 5:5

"Blessed are the meek: for they shall inherit the earth."
The meek are blessed and unique.

The meek are blessed and are not weak.

Matthew 4:10

I am in the Holy Ghost's divine praise and worship circuit.

To God my worship belongs.

(Matt. 7:7)

"Ask, and it shall be given you; seek, and ye shall find;
knock, and it shall be opened unto you:"
God's open door Satan cannot block.

All doors of opportunities I will knock.

(Mark 8:20)

Seven is God's perfect number from heaven.

I will populate heaven by using all my supernatural weapons.

(Philippians 4:6)

God heard all my unborn requests.

All my unborn gifts, talents, dreams, visions,
and revelations God will fulfill.

(Matthew 9:5–6)

Christ's power made my bed easy to carry.

Jesus Christ's power will empower every hour.

(Matt. 5:6)

"Blessed are they which do hunger and thirst after
righteousness: for they shall be filled."
Christ will beatify the meek and make us look younger.

The righteousness of God will exalt nations.

(Matt. 5:7)

"Blessed are the merciful: for they shall obtain mercy."
God's remnants are merciful and faithful.

God's remnants will be merciful to all nations.

(Matt. 5:8)

"Blessed are the pure in heart: for they shall see God."
My heart is pure, and in you I will soar like an eagle.

God, I will see you with my clean hands and pure heart.

"Blessed are the peacemakers: for they shall
be called the children of God."
We are God's peacemakers on earth.

We are God's peacemakers on earth to stop war makers.

(Ps. 1:6)

"For the LORD knoweth the way of the righteous:
but the way of the ungodly shall perish."
The way of the righteous should be cherished.

God's heaven is for us to inherit.

Psalm 1:4–5

The remnants will live for Christ and flourish.

Jesus Christ died for humanity that none will perish.

(Psalm 145:4–5)

The Holy Ghost is greater than fireworks.

Every generation will talk and sing of his magnificent works.

(Ps. 109:3)

"They compassed me about also with words of hatred;
and fought against me without a cause."
Love the Messiah's greatness toward us.

Hatred is from Satan and love is from God, so
hatred can never overpower love.

(Amos 3:3)

"Can two walk together, except they be agreed?"
Jesus Christ died, and the story is in the Bible, so read.

I am blessed to be a blessing, and this is my decree.

(Daniel 6)

In my lion's den, my story will be written with a pen.

My story with many dens of trouble will become my glory.

(Ezra 4:6)

My accusation is Jesus's application.

Satan's accusation will become his cremation.

(Neh. 4:6)

"So built we the wall; and all the wall was joined together
unto the half thereof: for the people had a mind to work."
Unity builds loving and peaceful communities.

Unity is a massive force to be reckoned with.

(John 10:10)

"The thief cometh not, but for to steal, and to kill,
and to destroy: I am come that they might have life,
and that they might have it more abundantly."
Satan comes to steal and make a deal.

Choose Christ and receive forgiveness, healing, and abundant life.

(Ruth 2:13)

Jesus Christ is my lifesaver, and he blesses me with great favor.

In Christ my labour is not in vain, and I am enjoying the heavenly rain.

(Lam. 3:20)

"My soul hath them still in remembrance, and is humbled in me."
I will be humble and not be ungrateful and grumble.

I am grateful for Christ's death on the cross for me.

(Lam. 3:22–24)

Nurses are always ready to show sympathy and mercy.

All humans need mercy, love, and compassion.

(Joshua 1:8)

Success can lead you to US Congress and to gain assets.

Success is great when shared with the poor and oppressed.

(Josh. 1:9)

"Have not I commanded thee? Be strong and of a good courage; be not afraid, neither be thou dismayed: for the LORD thy God is with thee whithersoever thou goest."
Joshua had courage and flourished.

Joshua was strong, and he won the battle with great success.

(Josh. 1:3)

"Every place that the sole of your foot shall tread upon,
that have I given unto you, as I said unto Moses."
Joshua was not defeated with God on his side.

Joshua, our God is never leaving.

(Ps. 4:8)

"I will both lay me down in peace, and sleep: for
thou, LORD, only makest me dwell in safety."
I will dwell in my bed with safety and sleep in peace.

God's peace is sweet and will never cease.

(Prov. 25:11)

"A word fitly spoken is like apples of gold in pictures of silver."
One positive word can stop depression at the root.

Just one fitly spoken word can change one's destiny.

(Prov. 24:1)

"Be not thou envious against evil men, neither desire to be with them."
An envious spirit leads to venomous actions.

Now is the time to replace envy, jealousy, and
covetousness with joy, happiness, and contentment.

(Prov. 25:13)

"As the cold of snow in the time of harvest, so is a faithful messenger
to them that send him: for he refresheth the soul of his masters."
My mind is refreshed by God's word.

The refreshing of God's holy words is worthy
and is our inheritance to invest.

(Prov. 25:19)

"Confidence in an unfaithful man in time of trouble
is like a broken tooth, and a foot out of joint."
In God lays my confidence, and this makes me competent.

The confidence of God enables us to do great exploits for him.

(Proverbs 25:21–22)

I will have mercy on and give water to the thirsty.

The ways of the Lord are love, peace, goodness, and mercy.

(Prov. 25:25)

"As cold waters to a thirsty soul, so is good news from a far country."
The gospel is the flooding of life changing good news.

The time is now to flood the earth with the
gospel of Jesus Christ good news.

(Prov. 27:5–6)

"Open rebuke is better than secret love. Faithful are the wounds
of a friend; but the kisses of an enemy are deceitful."
Spread the contagiousness of Christ's love.

Love is like an infection that can be transmitted.

(Prov. 26:27)

"Whoso diggeth a pit shall fall therein: and he that
rolleth a stone, it will return upon him."
There are benefits in God's divine planned pit.

The pit is God's perfectly designed plan for my blessings.

(Prov. 28:1)

"The wicked flee when no man pursueth: but
the righteous are bold as a lion."
I am bold and not cold and am designed with precious gold.

I am bold because Jehovah God is my stronghold.

(Ps. 27:1)

"The LORD is my light and my salvation; whom shall I fear? the
LORD is the strength of my life; of whom shall I be afraid?"
I will not be afraid because the Holy Ghost is my aid.

I will not fear the arrows that fly by day nor the pestilence
that walks in darkness because God is my protector.

(Ps. 91:10–11)

"There shall no evil befall thee, neither shall any plague
come nigh thy dwelling. For he shall give his angels
charge over thee, to keep thee in all thy ways."
I don't need to call an angel; mine is right beside me.

My assigned angels are watching over me twenty-
four seven, three hundred sixty five days a year.

(Ps. 91:13–14)

The devil's plan is for me to be trampled.

My feet have the power to trample the enemy every
hour because God is my strong tower.

(Psalm 91:15–16)

I will live long and in God be joyful, courageous, and strong.

I will live out all my days on this earth with
satisfaction and great contentment.

(Proverbs 28:19–20)

The blessing of the Lord comes with peace and
increase and will never decrease.

I will enjoy the blessings of the Lord and keep on pressing.

(Prov. 29:17)

"Correct thy son, and he shall give thee rest; yea,
he shall give delight unto thy soul."
A son is given by God with great might and delight.

The delight of a son changes the countenance of his parents.

(Ecclesiastes 12:1)

I have strength, so now I will serve my creator.

My creator gives me strength, and service from me is now required.

(Ecc. 1:7)

"All the rivers run into the sea; yet the sea is not full; unto the place from whence the rivers come, thither they return again."
The overflowing rivers and seas are all in God's control.

The rivers and seas are his, and they move or stand still at his command.

(Is. 66:18)

"For I know their works and their thoughts: it shall come, that I will gather all nations and tongues; and they shall come, and see my glory." Yeshua's majesty, glory, and power is my all-time story.

I will exalt Yeshua's majesty, glory, power, and dominion in the earth.

(Jer. 1:5)

"Before I formed thee in the belly I knew thee; and before
thou camest forth out of the womb I sanctified thee,
and I ordained thee a prophet unto the nations."
I am divinely planned by my creator.

I am divinely planned and divinely timed by my creator.

(Jer. 3:15)

"And I will give you pastors according to mine heart, which
shall feed you with knowledge and understanding."
I am a pastor called by the master with heart-mending plaster.

I am a pastor, and you can count on me to pray for victims of disasters.

(Jer. 30:17)

"For I will restore health unto thee, and I will heal thee of thy
wounds, saith the LORD; because they called thee an Outcast,
saying, This is Zion, whom no man seeketh after."
When I kneel to pray, I am healed and good I do feel.

By Jesus Christ's blood I am healed, and this he sealed.

(Jer. 30:22)

"And ye shall be my people, and I will be your God."
Your people shall see you greater than an eagle.

God's love for his people can be seen in his mysterious tome.

(Jeremiah 30:10–11)

Jacob believed that God would never leave.

To all Jews and Gentiles, God will never leave.

(Genesis 12:2–3)

The patriarch Abraham the great will always be celebrated.

God made Abraham great and his blessings were beyond any real estate.

(Jeremiah 33:11)

The voice of God makes me cheerful, hopeful, joyful, and grateful.

The voice of gladness and joy is my choice and to jump and rejoice

(Jer. 33:3)

"Call unto me, and I will answer thee, and show thee
great and mighty things, which thou knowest not."
Jehovah God is the Almighty, and he is all powerful and mighty.

"Jehovah God is omniscient and omnipresent."

(Eze. 3:22)

"And the hand of the LORD was there upon me; and he said unto me, Arise, go forth into the plain, and I will there talk with thee." I will arise as his chaste bride.

I will arise and shine, to the Holy Spirit I will be sensitized, and to win souls I will capitalize.

(Ps. 19:1)

"The heavens declare the glory of God; and the
firmament sheweth his handywork."
Look at me and you will see my master's divine beautiful artwork.

From the dust of the earth my creator created
me, and what perfect artwork.

(Psalm 19:7–8)

The blood of Jesus Christ is a cure for all for it does restore.

The blood of Jesus Christ will cure, mature, and endure.

(Psalm 19:9–10)

The word of God is more valuable than any gold mine.

Treasure the word of God as our gold mine.

(Ps. 19:14)

"Let the words of my mouth, and the meditation of my heart, be acceptable in thy sight, O LORD, my strength, and my redeemer."
On God's word I will meditate, it is my fate.

The word of God I will study, meditate, and be on Holy Ghost fire.

(Psalm 20:1–2)

Zion is on Holy Ghost fire and will aspire.

Zion is on Holy Ghost fire and is going higher.

(Psalm 20:3–4)

Giving my tithes and offering is a part of my calling.

Giving my tithes and offering, I will teach to my
offspring to praise and worship unto God.

(Psalm 79:11)

Christ is risen to deliver those who are in prison.

Christ is risen, and there is hope for those who are imprisoned.

(Psalm 22:26–27)

Now is the time to bow to God in humble adoration, praise, and honor.

All nations of the earth shall rise and worship
the creator of heaven and earth.

(Ps. 118:17)

"I shall not die, but live, and declare the works of the LORD."
The Holy Spirit has my life in overdrive to fulfill his work.

My former was good, but my latter will be greater.

(Luke 11:20)

"But if I with the finger of God cast out devils, no
doubt the kingdom of God is come upon you."
The finger of God is evident in my life.

The finger of God has written on all the pages of my life.

(2 Corinthians 13:4)

My weakness is God's strength.

In times of pain, grief, and sorrow, I am
infused with God's divine strength.

(Psalm 20:6–9)

All his anointed from birth are appointed.

I am called, chosen, anointed, and appointed
before the foundation of the earth.

(Ephesians 4:11–13)

Jehovah God will perfect and edify his church and his chosen people.

God's chosen people and the universal church are God's
watchtower that he will perfect with his power.

(Isaiah 40:29)

I take strength from Christ's empty tomb.

My strength is wrapped up in Jesus Christ's
death, burial, and resurrection.

(Matthew 16:13–18)

The son of the living God is not by flesh revealed.

The prayer of the righteous avails much and will prevail.

(Matthew 16:24–27)

Yes to Christ, yes to his love, and yes to his forgiveness.

When I say yes to Christ, I also say yes to his sufferings.

(Psalm 109:19–20)

My adversaries are God's responsibility.

My adversaries come to catapult me into my destiny.

(Psalm 107:20)

"He sent his word, and healed them, and delivered
them from their destructions."
By Christ's stripes I am healed, restored, and sealed.

Jesus Christ's stripes are scarified for my healing.

(Nahum 1:9)

"What do ye imagine against the LORD? he will make an utter end: affliction shall not rise up the second time." My afflictions are God's benediction.

The Holy Ghost's power is mightier in times of my afflictions.

(Ruth 2:12)

My rewards are God's award for me.

My rewards are in one accord with God.

(Ruth 1:16–17)

In God I will believe, cleave, and achieve.

The Holy Ghost I will not grieve but continue to perceive.

(Nehemiah 6:3)

Jesus Christ shed his blood for my good.

God's work is so great and enjoyable that I cannot come down.

(1 Kings 18:40–41)

The abundance of rain from the Holy Ghost will empower the saints.

I will be soaked in God's abundant rain.

(Heb. 11:1)

"Now faith is the substance of things hoped
for, the evidence of things not seen."
My hope in God is an eternal hope.

When I need hope I grab onto God's rope of hope.

(Heb. 11:6)

"But without faith it is impossible to please him: for he
that cometh to God must believe that he is, and that he
is a rewarder of them that diligently seek him."
Faith is believing that God will do what he promised.

My faith increases when I believe in the things I cannot see.

(Hebrews 11:24–26)

Christ's death gave me his friendship and fellowship.

Christ died for me—now that is called faithful.
Now it's my turn to live by faith in Christ.

(Hebrews 12:1–2)

Jesus Christ ran the race without looking back.

My eyes are set on Jesus Christ's ultimate price.

(Revelation 21:1–4)

The joy of heaven leaves no room for tears.

If heaven was like a stairwell, everyone would enter in,
but it is for his chosen people to eternally dwell.

(Genesis 12:3)

"And I will bless them that bless thee, and curse him that curseth
thee: and in thee shall all families of the earth be blessed."
It is my joy to bless and support the children of Israel.

Heaven is always on my mind because my life
is assigned and aligned to God's.

(John 10:10–11)

"The thief cometh not, but for to steal, and to kill, and to
destroy: I am come that they might have life, and that they
might have it more abundantly. I am the good shepherd:
the good shepherd giveth his life for the sheep."
God's sheep should be obedient and well kept.

Every night I pray for the sheep and go to sleep.

(Romans 15:6–7)

God's people should believe, cleave, perceive, and achieve.

To the word of God I will read, cleave, believe, perceive, and achieve.

(Judges 4:9)

Prophetess Deborah is a woman of great influence.

Deborah the prophetess, judge, counselor, songwriter,
and singer and all her praise was given to God.

(Judges 4:4–5)

God's gift of discernment is without prejudice.

Deborah discerned through the Holy Ghost and was
led by the Holy Ghost to deliver God's people.

(Esther 4:16)

Queen Esther gains favor and was cherished.

Queen Esther delivered her people; she was the
fairest, and her wages were not garnished.

(John 1:13-15)

God's love is beyond human comprehension and wisdom.

God loves us so much that he became a human being
and died on the cross for our trespasses and sins.

(Romans 15:1–2)

Show God's love, kindness, and goodness to our neighbors.

Love is a powerful force in the universe.

(Romans 15:15–16)

We should gossip about the goodness of Jesus Christ.

The gospel of Christ is awesome, and it should not just
be preached in the chapel but to the dying world.

(Philemon 1:3–6)

Having a heart of gratitude is better than having one million dollars.

I have a heart of gratitude, and this is greater than any bank.

(Philemon 1:20–21)

Make godly compassion a passion.

My compassion and passion are contagious like high fashion.

(Hosea 1:10–11)

God's love for Israel is greater than honey and the honeycomb.

God's blessings for his chosen people are supernatural and
extraordinary, and with this the Gentiles will agree.

(Hosea 2:21–22)

The Jews and Gentiles will preach the gospel of Christ.

The Jews and Gentiles will preach the gospel of
Jesus Christ, and the devil must disappear.

(Acts 13:2)

"As they ministered to the Lord, and fasted, the
Holy Ghost said, Separate me Barnabas and Saul for
the work whereunto I have called them."
Apostles, prophets, and prophetesses are God's elect.

The gospel of Jesus Christ is at stake. Let's preserve it for our eternity.

(Acts 13:16–18)

The Israelites' suffering ended, and God
accepted their sacrificial offerings.

The Israelites' suffering turns into supernatural discovery.

(Acts 13:29–30)

Jesus Christ rested for three days in his sepulchre.

Jesus Christ rested for three days in his sepulchre. Satan was at first glad, but he was unaware of the coming third-day resurrection triumph.

(1 Kings 17:1-5)

I hold dear the prophet Elijah's office.

I hold dear the prophet Elijah's office, and by
the Holy Ghost I will make progress.

(Colossians 1:9–10)

The Holy Spirit's knowledge is beyond any college.

The Holy Ghost's knowledge I acknowledge
for it makes the devil demolished.

(1 Thessalonians 2:3–5)

I was not an eyewitness, but I am an "I" witness for the Lord.

Being a witness for God, it is my business to recommend
his love, forgiveness, healing, and deliverance.

(1 Thessalonians 2:9–11)

I am God's laborer of love.

I am a laborer of love, and I know that my labor is not
in vain for his anointing, will fall on me like rain.

(1 Thess. 2:19-20)

"For what is our hope, or joy, or crown of rejoicing?
Are not even ye in the presence of our Lord Jesus Christ
at his coming? For ye are our glory and joy".
God's glory and joy are my congratulatory story.

I am injected and now infected with God's glory and joy.

(1Thessalonians 5:1–4)

I will not allow Satan to have me in disbelief.

My belief is in God for he is my chief.

(1 Thess. 5:5-6)

"Ye are all the children of light, and the children of the day:
we are not of the night, nor of darkness. Therefore let us
not sleep, as do others; but let us watch and be sober."
I was born for his delight.

My creator created me to illuminate the world with his light.

(1 Thessalonians 5:10–11)

Fly to all nations and with the gospel edify.

The gospel of Jesus Christ will edify humanity.

(1 Thessalonians 5:15–18)

My expression of appreciation to God is beyond a billion words.

Gratitude opens supernatural doors and goes beyond any human favors.

(1 Thess. 5:19–22)

"Quench not the Spirit. Despise not prophesyings. Prove all things;
hold fast that which is good. Abstain from all appearance of evil."
I will pray in the spirit for this will send Satan flying.

The Holy Spirit should not be quench. He
will give you unction to function.

(1 Thessalonians 5:24–28)

I was not just called by God but also anointed and appointed.

I am called, appointed, and anointed by God,
and this can cause Satan to be appalled.

(Prov. 18:10)

"The name of the LORD is a strong tower: the
righteous runneth into it, and is safe."
The Holy Ghost empowered me and gives me great power.

The Holy Ghost has the ultimate world power,
and he will always stay in power.

(Prov. 18:14-15)

"The spirit of a man will sustain his infirmity; but a wounded
spirit who can bear? The heart of the prudent getteth
knowledge; and the ear of the wise seeketh knowledge."
God's amazing grace will give you a true and cheerful spirit.

My countenance of joy will draw sinners to him.

(Proverbs 18:16)

"A man's gift maketh room for him, and
bringeth him before great men."
Activate your gift because it will open great doors,
and ushers you into the presence of the great.

My spiritual gifts will cause a shift and give me a lift, and this can be
seen on television in morning, during the day, and in the evening shift.

(Prov. 18:21)

"Death and life are in the power of the tongue: and
they that love it shall eat the fruit thereof."
I will live my life without strife.

My words will heal the sick and raise the death.

(Prov. 18:22)

"Whoso findeth a wife findeth a good thing,
and obtaineth favour of the LORD."
Your wife is God's favor because she will be your love chaser.

A wife is God's favor, so marry her without
wavering and all love memories do savor.

(Prov. 18:24)

"A man that hath friends must shew himself friendly: and
there is a friend that sticketh closer than a brother."
My friendliness is contagious and is so needed
in God's gospel general assembly.

Friendliness is a magnet that is needed on this planet.

(Obad. 1:17)

"But upon Mount Zion shall be deliverance, and there shall be holiness; and the house of Jacob shall possess their possessions."
Zion is moving forward with God's progression.

God has spoken that Zion will possess their possession and will not be depressed, distressed, nor oppressed.

(Matthew 11:25)

God's wisdom surpasses the wisdom of this world.

The revelation of heaven is spiritually discerned
and is given by the wisdom of God.

(Eph. 1:9–10)

"Having made known unto us the mystery of his will, according to his good pleasure which he hath purposed in himself: That in the dispensation of the fullness of times he might gather together in one all things in Christ, both which are in heaven, and which are on earth; even in him:"
The will of God is always perfect.

Let the perfect will of God be done in your life.

(1 John 5:14)

"And this is the confidence that we have in him, that, if we
ask any thing according to his will, he heareth us:"
God's divine confidence in me makes me competent.

His will is always perfect and will outdo the human will any day.

(Luke 4:18–19)

"The Spirit of the Lord is upon me, because he hath anointed me to preach the gospel to the poor; he hath sent me to heal the brokenhearted, to preach deliverance to the captives, and recovering of sight to the blind, to set at liberty them that are bruised, to preach the acceptable year of the Lord."
My evangelistic outreach is to teach and preach.

Jesus Christ's gospel I will teach, preach,
beseech, and outreach to each person.

(Micah 1:2–3)

God will tread upon the high places, and in the holy book it is read.

God will tread upon the high places of the earth,
so prepare praise and worship ahead.

(Micah 7:5)

"Trust ye not in a friend, put ye not confidence in a guide: keep
the doors of thy mouth from her that lieth in thy bosom."
My mouth will confess that in you I put my trust.

God is constant and will never leave me.

(Micah 7:7–8)

"Therefore I will look unto the LORD; I will wait for the
God of my salvation: my God will hear me. Rejoice not
against me, O mine enemy: when I fall, I shall arise; when
I sit in darkness, the LORD shall be a light unto me."
I shall not die, but at my destination I will safely arrive.

With the Holy Ghost's power I will arise, baptize, give
sound advice, and overcome all the enemy's devices.

(Mark 14)

All my trespasses and sin he took to Gethsemane's garden.

Only God is the true judge of heaven and
earth. He is called the God of justice.

(Micah 7:20)

"Thou wilt perform the truth to Jacob, and the mercy to Abraham,
which thou hast sworn unto our fathers from the days of old."
The God of Abraham, Isaac, and Jacob will bless you.

In this life, there is no need to stress and brainstorm
because God will supernaturally perform.

(1 Samuel 30:18–20)

I will recover and rediscover all things that Satan has under cover.

My restoration is now in every location and habitation of the earth.

(2 Samuel 5:3–4)

God reign for all eternity so I plan to reign with him.

God is our immortal, invisible, only wise God that will
stand one day upon this earth and will reign eternally.

(2 Sam. 5:7)

"Nevertheless David took the strong hold of
Zion: the same is the city of David."
Zion will prevail, and all is told in the Bible.

The Holy Ghost's power will reign in the body of Christ, and
we will see the manifestation of the fivefold ministry.

(2 Sam. 5:19)

"And David enquired of the LORD, saying, Shall I go
up to the Philistines? wilt thou deliver them into mine
hand? And the LORD said unto David, Go up: for I will
doubtless deliver the Philistines into thine hand."
To God I will inquire for his solution that will never expire.

In all that I do, I will inquire of the Lord because this is
important and is required for my decisive victory.

(2 Sam. 5:25)

"And David did so, as the LORD had commanded him; and
smote the Philistines from Geba until thou come to Gazer."
David smote the Israelites' enemies, and to God he was devoted.

The Holy Ghost is our antidote for all of our enemies.

(1 Samuel 18:7)

Watch out because jealousy comes from every corner of life.

The decisive victory that God gave his chosen people gave Saul misery.

(1 Sam. 18:12–14)

"And Saul was afraid of David, because the LORD was with him, and was departed from Saul. Therefore Saul removed him from him, and made him his captain over a thousand; and he went out and came in before the people. And David behaved himself wisely in all his ways; and the LORD was with him."
God favored David, but Saul was vexed.

God will give me a triumphant victory and
perplex and defeat my enemies.

(1 Samuel 18:28–29)

With God I am spiritually fit to outrun my enemies.

The Lord is on my side so victory is mine. I will get
my heritage slice, and Satan will be shocked.

(Hab. 2:3–4)

"For the vision is yet for an appointed time, but at the end it shall
speak, and not lie: though it tarry, wait for it; because it will
surely come, it will not tarry. Behold, his soul which is lifted
up is not upright in him: but the just shall live by his faith."
My vision from God will be seen on television.

My vision from God will be seen on television
for God is my providential provision.

"But the LORD is in his holy temple: let all
the earth keep silence before him."
God is the roaring lion, and yet he is the lamb in my silence.

When the lion of the tribe of Judah roars it draws attention to the world.

(Habakkuk 3:1–2)

God is merciful to all those who are oppressed.

God's mercy is everlasting and can be trusted.

(James 1:5–9)

Wisdom is from the supreme power, and that is God.

Let us be steadfast and unmovable in God, for with
an unsteady mind, Satan is always ready.

(Acts 9:11–12)

I need my sight to see day, evening, and night.

My sight is my spiritual right, and God's healing is not
by might nor by the power but by the Holy Ghost.

(Acts 9:31)

"Then had the churches rest throughout all Judaea and Galilee and Samaria, and were edified; and walking in the fear of the Lord, and in the comfort of the Holy Ghost, were multiplied."
I will fear God and make him part of my career.

The Holy Ghost's power is our deliverer in every hour.

(Acts 9:39–42)

Tabitha is raised from the dead, and the
apostle Peter was given a high five.

Tabitha arose by the power the Holy Ghost invested in
the apostle Peter. Now the devil takes a dive.

(Acts 12:5)

"Peter therefore was kept in prison: but prayer was made
without ceasing of the church unto God for him."
I will call heaven for my secret weapon.

Prayer is one of our earthly weapons that will destroy
the enemies, for victory we shall enjoy.

(1 Cor. 16:9)

"For a great door and effectual is opened unto
me, and there are many adversaries."
From my door of distinction, blessings will outpour.

God has divine blessings and prosperity for me in store.

(1 Cor. 16:13–14)

"Watch ye, stand fast in the faith, quit you like men, be
strong. Let all your things be done with charity."
Charity can turn you into a celebrity.

Familiarity breeds contempt, but charity can give us serenity.

(1 Cor. 16:1–2)

"Now concerning the collection for the saints, as I have given
order to the churches of Galatia, even so do ye. Upon the first
day of the week let every one of you lay by him in store, as God
hath prospered him, that there be no gatherings when I come."
Giving my tithes and offering, I am honoring God.

When I give my tithes and offering, I am a partaker of Christ's suffering.

(1 Peter 2:23)

The word of God is without apology.

God's word is pure, rich, wealthy, unchangeable, and unstoppable.

(2 Peter 3:18)

"But grow in grace, and in the knowledge of our Lord and Saviour
Jesus Christ. To him be glory both now and forever. Amen."
God's grace is for all shame, guilt, and disgrace.

God's grace is so divine that it will erase and
forgive all sins and then embrace.

(1 Peter 1:18–19)

"The spotless lamb was rated highly by Abraham."

Jesus Christ was the perfect spotless lamb given
to this world by his heavenly Father.

(Romans 3:24–25)

The word of God is made plain for all to understand it.

The word of God is the perfect cure for all of life's
situations, problems, and circumstances.

(1 Peter. 1:13)

"Wherefore gird up the loins of your mind, be sober,
and hope to the end for the grace that is to be brought
unto you at the revelation of Jesus Christ;"
The saints will have the mind of Christ.

The mind of Christ is not confined but is infinitely refined.

(Num. 6:23–26)

"Speak unto Aaron and unto his sons, saying, On this wise ye shall bless the children of Israel, saying unto them, The LORD bless thee, and keep thee: The LORD make his face shine upon thee, and be gracious unto thee: The LORD lift up his countenance upon thee, and give thee peace."
God's peace is my divine peace.

My peace in God, Satan will not decrease but daily increase.

(2 John 2:2)

"For the truth's sake, which dwelleth in us, and shall be with us forever."
The beginning and ending of all truth is God.

The truth of God will manifest in all darkness.

(2 John 3:3)

"Grace be with you, mercy, and peace, from God the Father, and from the Lord Jesus Christ, the Son of the Father, in truth and love." The God of love is a peaceful dove.

Love is not without giving. God gave his only begotten son for humanity.

(1 John 3:7)

"Little children, let no man deceive you: he that doeth
righteousness is righteous, even as he is righteous."
God's righteousness comes with brightness.

The righteousness of God is rightness.

(Mathew 6:10)

"Thy kingdom come, Thy will be done in earth, as it is in heaven."
Ask God according to his will, and you will have a thrill.

God's will is the perfect will for us, but we still have free will.

(1 John 3:2)

Only God knows what we shall be in the end, so cheers.

The beginning of fear is knowing God, knowing God gives us humility.

(1 Corinthians 13:1–2)

God's love is the perfect gift all season.

Our heavenly Father's gift to mankind is not
perishable and not corruptible.

(1 Cor. 13:8-9)

"Charity never faileth: but whether there be prophecies, they shall fail; whether there be tongues, they shall cease; whether there be knowledge, it shall vanish away. For we know in part, and we prophesy in part."
God's love is never on sale. There's no need to line up—it is free.

God's infinite love toward me is sufficient for me in this life.

(1 Cor. 13:13)

"And now abideth faith, hope, charity, these three;
but the greatest of these is charity."
Love is an expression of giving.

Love is an act of giving; it is better to give than to receive.

(1 Corinthians 12:4–7)

The Holy Ghost's manifestation is his solid foundation.

The manifestation of the Holy Ghost is without
apology against all enemies' accusations.

(1 Corinthians 12:25–27)

To love and honor one another is part of our calling.

When God's love is expressed within the body of
Christ, we are a force to be reckoned with.

(1 Corinthians 12:28–31)

My gift from God is without repentance,
and there is no need for apology.

My gift will take me to nations and give me uplift; to God I will stick.

(1 Cor. 10:26)

"For the earth is the Lord's, and the fullness thereof."
All that is in this world belongs to the heavenly Father.

This world's goods and possessions are mine
because this is my heavenly Father's world.

(1 Cor. 9:13)

"Do ye not know that they which minister about holy
things live of the things of the temple? and they which
wait at the altar are partakers with the altar?"
Fasting and prayer were the apostles' temple weapons.

The apostles preached daily the good news of Jesus,
and providential provision was given to them.

(Ps. 8:2)

"Out of the mouth of babes and sucklings hast thou
ordained strength because of thine enemies, that thou
mightest still the enemy and the avenger."
Babes are precious and are loved greatly by God.

The mouths of babes will utter supernatural
mysteries of God and the heavens.

(Ps. 8:4–6)

God's dominion he gave to man over the works of his hands.

God's dominion is not Satan's opinion.

(Ps. 8:9)

"O Lord, our Lord, how excellent is thy name in all the earth!"
God created us from the dust of the earth, so we should adjust.

Lord most high your name is excellent in all the earth.

(John 16:14–15)

"He shall glorify me: for he shall receive of mine, and shall shew
it unto you. All things that the Father hath are mine: therefore
said I, that he shall take of mine, and shall shew it unto you."
God is worthy to be glorified.

The more we glorify God, the richer his presence in our lives becomes.

(John 16:33)

"These things I have spoken unto you, that in me ye
might have peace. In the world ye shall have tribulation:
but be of good cheer; I have overcome the world."
Be of good cheer; God is always near.

I will glorify God in fifth gear.

(John 16:23)

"And in that day ye shall ask me nothing. Verily, verily, I say unto you,
Whatsoever ye shall ask the Father in my name, he will give it you."
In Jesus' name, my blessings I will claim.

In Jesus' name, all that the enemy has stolen I will reclaim.

(Mark 10:39)

I share in Christ's baptism and his suffering.

Every day the name of Jesus Christ is criticized by the enemy,
yet his name is the most powerful name on earth.

(John 4:23-24)

"But the hour cometh, and now is, when the true worshippers shall worship the Father in spirit and in truth: for the Father seeketh such to worship him. God is a Spirit: and they that worship him must worship him in spirit and in truth." Authentic worship can only be true in spirit and in truth.

When I worship God in spirit and in truth, his awesome presence becomes tangible.

(John 4:25–26)

God's words are true as can be and always win gold.

God's words can enter any contest and must win
gold because his words are infinite truth.

(John 4:15)

"The woman saith unto him, Sir, give me this water,
that I thirst not, neither come hither to draw."
His water quenches my thirst and leaves me in awe.

His living water is the best for all situations.

(Judges 6:12)

"And the angel of the LORD appeared unto him, and said unto
him, The LORD is with thee, thou mighty man of valour."
Having the presence of the Lord with me
helps me overcome all my fears.

Even in my valley, I believe that God is still my master.

(Romans 1:20)

God is supernaturally powerful.

I am a carrier of the Holy Ghost's firepower.

(John 4:10)

"Jesus answered and said unto her, If thou knewest the gift of God, and who it is that saith to thee, Give me to drink; thou wouldest have asked of him, and he would have given thee living water."
His water comes from a supernatural source.

His water comes from a supernatural source that has effective solutions and no contamination.

(Matthew 5:13)

I am the salt of the earth and Christ I will exalt.

I will give flavor to the earth and bring glory to his name.

(Mark 5:7–9)

The most high God's authority is final in deliverance.

Legion must be subjected to the authority of the most high God.

(Mark 4:11–12)

At Calvary's cross is where our sins are forgiven.

At Calvary's cross is where freedom begins.

(Mark 4:39)

"And he arose, and rebuked the wind, and said unto the sea, Peace, be still. And the wind ceased, and there was a great calm."
Humankind's wind is God pleasure to calm.

The wind of life will be calmed by the authoritative voice of God.

(Mark 4:41)

"And they feared exceedingly, and said one to another, What manner of man is this, that even the wind and the sea obey him?" God's voice is assigned to all of our contrary wind.

The voice of God will calm my wind and give me peace of mind.

(Heb. 6:13–14)

"For when God made promise to Abraham, because he could swear by no greater, he sware by himself, Saying, Surely blessing I will bless thee, and multiplying I will multiply thee."
I am blessed without distress.

I am blessed with success to progress forward.

(Hebrews 7:1–2)

My creator gave me two hands. I will use one hand to give to those in need and the other to receive the blessings of the Lord.

By giving my tenth part of all, I will have access
to open doors of great opportunities.

(Psalm 40:5)

God's infinite thoughts toward me are great and numberless.

You are wonderful in all your works, and your blessings can
never be outnumbered because you never slumber.

(Hebrews 6:18)

God is our immutable refuge and strong consolation.

Because God is immutable, I have confidence in all his promises.

(Num. 23:19–20)

"God is not a man, that he should lie; neither the son of man, that he should repent: hath he said, and shall he not do it? or hath he spoken, and shall he not make it good? Behold, I have received commandment to bless: and he hath blessed; and I cannot reverse it." I am a registered nurse. I am blessed, and no one can curse.

I am blessed and able to converse, and no one can curse.

(Is. 26:4)

"Trust ye in the LORD for ever: for in the LORD
JEHOVAH is everlasting strength:"
My God is just and trustworthy, and his will I will follow.

In God I trust for Satan is unjust and unrighteous.

"As for God, his way is perfect: the word of the LORD is tried: he is a buckler to all those that trust in him. For who is God save the LORD? or who is a rock save our God?" Jesus Christ is my solid rock that Satan's tricks cannot knock.

On Christ Jesus' rock I stand for his flock I must guide.

(Is. 60:19)

Jesus Christ is right all the time for he is the eternal light.

Jesus Christ is the brightest light in the day, evening, and night.

(2 Sam. 7:28)

"And now, O Lord God, thou art that God, and thy words be true, and thou hast promised this goodness unto thy servant:" My right hand is full of God's divine promises.

God will surely show me his goodness, and I believe in his sureness and pureness.

(John 15:13)

"Greater love hath no man than this, that a man
lay down his life for his friends."
Jesus Christ is my pure and righteous friend
from the beginning until the end.

Jesus Christ is a true friend that I can depend on
and will extend his love and not pretend.

(Psalm 93:3–5)

God has blessed all my endeavors wherever I go.

God will protect me against the enemy's terror.

(2 Sam. 22:34)

"He maketh my feet like hinds' feet: and
setteth me upon my high places."
God has given me hinds' feet and his word to subdue Satan.

God is higher than all my mountains; his grace
will keep me in this gospel race.

(Prov. 27:4)

"Wrath is cruel, and anger is outrageous; but
who is able to stand before envy?"
Envy is wicked, and it can destroy you.

Envy is not friendly for it will take you to the grave.

(Prov. 14:30)

"A sound heart is the life of the flesh: but
envy the rottenness of the bones."
Jesus Christ was the rejected stone, but he
was exalted to his Father's throne.

Jesus Christ's power turn stumbling blocks into stepping stones.

(Prov. 20:25)

"It is a snare to the man who devoureth that which
is holy, and after vows to make enquiry."
Holiness is God's requirement for those who want to see him.

Holiness is not noisiness and sometimes can cause loneliness.

(James 1:1–4)

When we go through our fiery darks, this builds character in us.

Our fiery darks make us stronger, wiser, braver, and more courageous.

(Ps. 34:19)

"Many are the afflictions of the righteous: but the
LORD delivereth him out of them all."
Our afflictions will lead us to the crucifixion.

Our afflictions will turn us into mathematicians.

(1 Cor. 1:9)

"God is faithful, by whom ye were called unto the
fellowship of his Son Jesus Christ our Lord."
Our fellowship with Christ Jesus will give us peace and serenity.

Fellowship and sweet communion with Jesus Christ are rewarding.

(Deut. 32:4)

"He is the Rock, his work is perfect: for all his ways are judgment:
a God of truth and without iniquity, just and right is he."
When I stand on the rock of Christ Jesus, the devil cannot mock.

I will stand on the solid rock of Jesus Christ and
praise him right around the clock.

(Jer. 29:11)

"For I know the thoughts that I think toward you, saith the LORD, thoughts of peace, and not of evil, to give you an expected end."
I will build my life upon the perfect plans of God.

God's plans for my life are perfect and will
continue throughout my life span.

(Ps. 16:5)

"The LORD is the portion of mine inheritance and
of my cup: thou maintainest my lot."
I will trust the Lord as my portion inheritance,
for it will not come to naught.

I have irreversible blessings from the Lord.

(Prov. 19:20)

"Hear counsel, and receive instruction, that
thou mayest be wise in thy latter end."
I am not wise in my own eyes, but in God's eyes I am.

The wisdom of humans will capsize, but God's wisdom will nationalize.

(Matt. 5:44)

"But I say unto you, Love your enemies, bless them that
curse you, do good to them that hate you, and pray for
them which despitefully use you, and persecute you."
It is the plan of the devil to persecute us, but God will uproot his plans.

God is always en route to take root for his people.

(1 Cor. 2:9)

"But as it is written, Eye hath not seen, nor ear heard,
neither have entered into the heart of man, the things
which God hath prepared for them that love him."
Every day I arise and look forward to his surprise.

God's glorious surprise Satan cannot outsize.

(Rom. 15:30)

"Now I beseech you, brethren, for the Lord Jesus
Christ's sake, and for the love of the Spirit, that ye strive
together with me in your prayers to God for me;"
Together let us live in peace and increase peace.

When the peace of God is increased, then war will cease.

(Luke 14:26)

"If any man come to me, and hate not his father, and
mother, and wife, and children, and brethren, and sisters,
yea, and his own life also, he cannot be my disciple."
Deny yourself take up your cross, follow him and frustrate the enemies.

Love is the opposite of hate, so let's love instead of hate.

(Rom. 13:8)

"Owe no man anything, but to love one another: for
he that loveth another hath fulfilled the law."
Loving one another will bring peace and joy in our lives.

Loving one another is the strong bond that
will break the enemy's chains.

(2 Peter 1:5-7)

"And beside this, giving all diligence, add to your faith virtue; and to virtue knowledge; And to knowledge temperance; and to temperance patience; and to patience godliness; And to godliness brotherly kindness; and to brotherly kindness charity."
When I love the unlovable, I am fulfilling God's commandment of love.

Love the unlovable, and null and void Satan's destruction.

(1 Thess. 4:9)

"But as touching brotherly love ye need not that I write unto you: for ye yourselves are taught of God to love one another." Love is the cornerstone for any relationship.

Love is the greatest force in the universe.

(Prov. 22:6)

"Train up a child in the way he should go: and
when he is old, he will not depart from it."
Feed children's brains with the word of God, and in life they will reign.

Train children well, and their labor will not be in
vain and steadfast minds they will maintain.

(Prov. 4:7)

"Wisdom is the principal thing; therefore get wisdom:
and with all thy getting get understanding."
Give me understanding, Lord, and I will fulfill my destiny.

Give me understanding, and it will advance every area of my life.

(Matt. 6:33)

"But seek ye first the kingdom of God, and his righteousness;
and all these things shall be added unto you."
I put God first, and he gave me outbursts of blessings.

I put God first, and I am a blessing that no one can curse.

(Zech. 4:6)

"Then he answered and spake unto me, saying, This is the word of the LORD unto Zerubbabel, saying, Not by might, nor by power, but by my spirit, saith the LORD of hosts."

The Holy Spirit is not a gimmick, and he has no limit.

The Holy Spirit will visit and keep us in high spirits.

(Matt. 11:28–30)

"Come unto me, all ye that labour and are heavy laden, and I
will give you rest. Take my yoke upon you, and learn of me;
for I am meek and lowly in heart: and ye shall find rest unto
your souls. For my yoke is easy, and my burden is light."
I give my heavy burdens to the Lord, and he breaks my every yoke.

Jesus Christ is my burden bearer and yoke destroyer.

(Eph. 2:10)

"For we are his workmanship, created in Christ Jesus unto good works, which God hath before ordained that we should walk in them." I am God's workmanship with no guilt trip.

I am God's workmanship that will excel in leadership.

(Rev. 4:11)

"Thou art worthy, O Lord, to receive glory and
honour and power: for thou hast created all things, and
for thy pleasure they are and were created."
I am uniquely created to love and relate and not hate.

I am created by my creator to activate my gifts.

(Acts 22:16)

"And now why tarriest thou? arise, and be baptized, and wash away thy sins, calling on the name of the Lord."
I will arise and shine for I am swifter than eagles.

I will arise, shine, and memorize daily the word of God.

(Gal. 3:27)

"For as many of you as have been baptized
into Christ have put on Christ."
I believe in Jesus Christ, baptized and now I am a new creature.

The Holy Ghost's power will help me to pass through my valleys.

(Romans 10:8–10)

Accept Jesus Christ, confess your sins, and this will lead to salvation.

Salvation takes away frustration and gives you cause for celebration.

(Is. 55:6–7)

"Seek ye the LORD while he may be found, call ye upon him while he is near: Let the wicked forsake his way, and the unrighteous man his thoughts: and let him return unto the LORD, and he will have mercy upon him; and to our God, for he will abundantly pardon."
Jesus Christ will pardon our sins and set us free from burdens.

Jesus Christ will pardon, so do not harden your heart.

(Eph. 2:8–9)

"For by grace are ye saved through faith; and that not of yourselves:
it is the gift of God: Not of works, lest any man should boast."
Jesus Christ's death gave me embracing grace, not disgrace.

The grace of God my sins erase, and freedom has taken place.

(James 2:24)

"Ye see then how that by works a man is justified, and not by faith only."
The saints of old had great faith that destroyed Satan's bait.

When the saints do God's good work on
earth, it is greater than fireworks.

(Rom. 5:8)

"But God commendeth his love toward us, in that,
while we were yet sinners, Christ died for us."
Jesus Christ died for humanity, and his blood can apply to every case.

Jesus Christ died for sinners, and he gives us
inner peace that makes us winners.

(1 Cor. 1:18)

"For the preaching of the cross is to them that perish foolishness;
but unto us which are saved it is the power of God."
I believe in the cross, and I will never be lost.

The cross of Jesus Christ I will cherish, and I will
spread it to those who are perishing.

(Mark 15:29–30)

The cross of Jesus Christ Satan despises for it
is given to humanity not to perish.

The cross of Jesus Christ is caring, loving, sharing, and embracing.

(Mark 8:34)

"And when he had called the people unto him with his disciples
also, he said unto them, Whosoever will come after me, let
him deny himself, and take up his cross, and follow me."
My self-denial to follow Christ has great eternal rewards.

Follow Jesus Christ, believe his words, apply his
words, and your spiritual life won't be shallow.

(Heb. 12:2)

"Looking unto Jesus the author and finisher of our faith; who for the joy that was set before him endured the cross, despising the shame, and is set down at the right hand of the throne of God." God is sitting on his throne, and he will crown his own.

Jesus Christ, the chief cornerstone, is well known.

(Is. 9:6)

"For unto us a child is born, unto us a son is given: and
the government shall be upon his shoulder: and his name
shall be called Wonderful, Counsellor, The mighty God,
The everlasting Father, The Prince of Peace."
Jesus Christ, our wisest counselor, has every area of our lives covered.

Jesus Christ won the award as the miraculous prince of peace.

(1 Peter 2:24–25)

The bishop of our soul will never grow old nor leave us in the cold.

The bishop of our souls will help us to establish our goals.

(Is. 53:5)

"But he was wounded for our transgressions, he was
bruised for our iniquities: the chastisement of our peace
was upon him; and with his stripes we are healed."
I will kneel in prayer and believe that by his stripes I am healed.

By his stripes I am healed, and his word he revealed.

(Ps. 22:22)

"I will declare thy name unto my brethren: in the
midst of the congregation will I praise thee."
I will praise the name of Jesus always and every day.

When I pray and believe, his results are incredible.

(1 Peter 1:21)

"Who by him do believe in God, that raised him up from the dead,
and gave him glory; that your faith and hope might be in God."
I am enveloped in the love of God.

Jesus Christ rose from the dead, and this means that
I am now able to cope with my situations.

(John 10:10)

"The thief cometh not, but for to steal, and to kill,
and to destroy: I am come that they might have life,
and that they might have it more abundantly."
In God I will dwell for the enemy's attack is relentless.

I am dwelling in God's secret place, and I will enjoy abundant joy.

(Rom. 3:23)

"For all have sinned, and come short of the glory of God;"
Sin began in the Garden of Eden with Adam and Eve.

Sin looks appealing, but the end of it is eternal bitterness.

(Rom. 14:11)

"For it is written, As I live, saith the Lord, every knee shall
bow to me, and every tongue shall confess to God."
Salvation is free, so why not kneel and accept Christ's deal?

Christ was hung upon a tree just for humanity to be set free.

(Is. 53:6)

"All we like sheep have gone astray; we have turned every one to his own way; and the LORD hath laid on him the iniquity of us all."
With Christ as my captain, I will never sink
because he will calm the storm.

Only the Lord Jesus Christ could have borne such pain
and agony for humanity to live and have eternal life.

(Phil. 3:10)

"That I may know him, and the power of his resurrection, and the fellowship of his sufferings, being made conformable unto his death."
Jesus Christ's resurrection brings holiness and perfection.

Jesus Christ's resurrection power gives connection and completion.

(Is. 63:1)

"Who is this that cometh from Edom, with dyed garments from
Bozrah? this that is glorious in his apparel, travelling in the greatness
of his strength? I that speak in righteousness, mighty to save."
God's amazing grace delivers us eternally from the grave.

God's grace has set me free, and I am no longer enslaved.

(Acts 5:31)

"Him hath God exalted with his right hand to be a Prince and a Saviour, for to give repentance to Israel, and forgiveness of sins."
God's amazing grace is sufficient for all nations.

God loves us, and he gave us his blameless lamb.

(1 John 3:8)

"He that committeth sin is of the devil; for the devil sinneth
from the beginning. For this purpose the Son of God was
manifested, that he might destroy the works of the devil."
The devil was thrown out of heaven because he lost the war in heaven.

God alone rules the heavens and the earth,
and it will be this way for eternity.

(Mark 16:17–18)

The sick will recover because Satan's plan was discovered.

God's word brings healing because the Holy Spirit always hovers.

(John 1:1)

"In the beginning was the Word, and the Word
was with God, and the Word was God."
The word of God is my permanent weapon,
so I will gird it around my loins.

The word of God is my permanent GPS in this life.

(John 1:14)

"And the Word was made flesh, and dwelt among
us, (and we beheld his glory, the glory as of the only
begotten of the Father,) full of grace and truth."
The word of God is precious and miraculous
when it takes root inside my heart.

The word of God I will teach to today's youth so they
will know the only truth, which is Jesus Christ.

(Is. 26:3)

"Thou wilt keep him in perfect peace, whose mind is
stayed on thee: because he trusteth in thee."
God's peace is calming and reassuring.

I leave behind my heavy load, and I take up God's wonderful peace.

(Ps. 16:11)

"Thou wilt shew me the path of life: in thy presence is fullness
of joy; at thy right hand there are pleasures for evermore."
In his presence, all evil is destroyed and there is boundless joy to enjoy.

The presence of the Lord is incredible and magnificent.

(Is. 61:7)

"For your shame ye shall have double; and for confusion they shall rejoice in their portion: therefore in their land they shall possess the double: everlasting joy shall be unto them."
For humanity's shame God will give us double blessings.

God's grace erases our past and gives us new beginnings.

(Ps. 32:8)

"I will instruct thee and teach thee in the way which
thou shalt go: I will guide thee with mine eye."
He will guide me with his eye, and yes, he sees me when I cry.

His eye is powerful; he is watching the heavens and the earth.

(Rom. 4:25)

"Who was delivered for our offences, and was
raised again for our justification."
We get justification for our frustration.

Satan gives accusation and complication, and Jesus
Christ gives justification and celebration.

(Rom. 10:9–10)

"That if thou shalt confess with thy mouth the Lord Jesus, and shalt believe in thine heart that God hath raised him from the dead, thou shalt be saved. For with the heart man believeth unto righteousness; and with the mouth confession is made unto salvation."
Confession leads to conversion, and conversation is full salvation.

Salvation delivers humanity from stagnation and exploitation and leads us to our heavenly destination.

(Ps. 103:2–4)

"Bless the LORD, O my soul, and forget not all his benefits:Who
forgiveth all thine iniquities; who healeth all thy diseases;
Who redeemeth thy life from destruction; who crowneth
thee with lovingkindness and tender mercies;"
Lovingkindness + tender mercies = infinite goodness.

His tender mercies are new every morning, and I will
praise and worship him twenty-four seven.

(Jer. 17:14)

"Heal me, O Lord, and I shall be healed; save me,
and I shall be saved: for thou art my praise."
God's praise deserves a raise and is worth a blaze.

I will activate the praise and worship alarm.

(Jer. 33:6)

"Behold, I will bring it health and cure, and I will cure them,
and will reveal unto them the abundance of peace and truth."
The blameless lamb was pure, and he is still the cure that will endure.

Jesus Christ endures the cross to give divine security.

(James 5:15)

"And the prayer of faith shall save the sick, and the Lord shall raise him up; and if he have committed sins, they shall be forgiven him."
Read God's word + pray + believe = heaven solution.

Humble + pray + turn + believe = healing solution.

(3 John 1:2)

"Beloved, I wish above all things that thou mayest prosper
and be in health, even as thy soul prospereth."
I will be in good health and prosper in all my life's endeavors.

I declare and decree divine prosperity and serenity over my life.

(Prov. 20:1)

"Wine is a mocker, strong drink is raging: and
whosoever is deceived thereby is not wise."
I will not give heed to strong drink but stay
intoxicated in God's presence.

Strong drink is raging and causes damage to the brain and agonizing
consequences in life, so staying sober means that you are wise.

(Gal. 5:1)

"Stand fast therefore in the liberty wherewith Christ hath made us free, and be not entangled again with the yoke of bondage." When I acknowledged Jesus Christ as my personal Lord and Savior, I came out of bondage.

Be free from the bondage of sin and shame and gain advantage of kingdom knowledge.

(Phil. 2:5)

"Let this mind be in you, which was also in Christ Jesus:"
With a godly mind-set I am perfectly fine and will help others to align.

It is the plan of Satan to keep our minds confined, but it
is the plan of God to keep our minds unconfined.

(1 Cor. 6:19–20)

"What? know ye not that your body is the temple of the Holy
Ghost which is in you, which ye have of God, and ye are not
your own? For ye are bought with a price: therefore glorify
God in your body, and in your spirit, which are God's."
My body is the temple of the Lord, and I am a vessel of honor.

I am a special temple of the Lord, and in God's holy presence
I tremble. And I will not allow Satan to dissemble.

(Heb. 13:4)

"Marriage is honourable in all, and the bed undefiled:
but whoremongers and adulterers God will judge."
Marriage is God's institution that is honorable and admirable.

Marriage is honorable, and in the end only
God will be the ultimate judge.

(Gal. 1:10)

"For do I now persuade men, or God? or do I seek to please men?
for if I yet pleased men, I should not be the servant of Christ."
Please God and be meek, or please men and be weak.

Pleasing God first makes me unique, and for God I will speak.

(Rom. 12:2)

"And be not conformed to this world: but be ye transformed
by the renewing of your mind, that ye may prove what is
that good, and acceptable, and perfect, will of God."
Being conformed to this world will make me
lukewarm and not transformed.

Being conformed to this world will only give me
rainstorms, firestorms, and thunderstorms.

(1 Cor. 15:33–34)

"Be not deceived: evil communications corrupt good manners.
Awake to righteousness, and sin not; for some have not
the knowledge of God: I speak this to your shame."
Do not live your life with shame, but instead
claim salvation and gain freedom.

Satan will give you the shame game, but choose
God and he will give you a new name.

(Romans 12:19)

"Dearly beloved, avenge not yourselves, but rather give place unto wrath: for it is written, Vengeance is mine; I will repay, saith the Lord." I will not avenge because this will only lead to revenge.

On God I depend for he will avenge.

(Matthew 7:1)

I will not judge but pay close attention to the Holy Spirit's nudge.

Judging leads to misjudging and then to begrudging.

(Matthew 5:44)

Blessings will put money in my purse.

I will love those who despitefully use me and get reimbursed blessings.

(Eph. 3:20)

"Now unto him that is able to do exceeding abundantly above all that we ask or think, according to the power that worketh in us," God is capable of doing for us unthinkable miracles.

God is supreme and is able to do for us what we cannot do for ourselves.

(Matt. 18:18)

"Verily I say unto you, Whatsoever ye shall bind on
earth shall be bound in heaven: and whatsoever ye
shall loose on earth shall be loosed in heaven."
My mind is loose to the freedom of God.

I declare God's blessings and prosperity in
my life right now in Jesus' name.

(Ps. 51:1–2)

"Have mercy upon me, O God, according to thy
lovingkindness: according unto the multitude of thy tender
mercies blot out my transgressions. Wash me thoroughly
from mine iniquity, and cleanse me from my sin."
I am washed in the blood of Jesus Christ and
will not allow Satan to squash me.

God's forgiveness is his lovingkindness and mercy toward me.

(Prov. 27:17)

"Iron sharpeneth iron; so a man sharpeneth
the countenance of his friend."
My friends sharpened my countenance and gave me a praise garment.

The sharpening of my countenance is like a beautiful garden.

(Exo. 20:3)

"Thou shalt have no other Gods before me."
The worshipers of false gods will always find fault.

I will worship God and memorize my Bible verses.

(Psalm 135:15–18)

Humankind's idols will eventually be their trials.

Humankind's idols do not give satisfaction or revival.

(Ps. 18:29)

"For by thee I have run through a troop; and by
my God have I leaped over a wall."
All my walls will come down just like the one at Jericho.

My walls are never stronger than my God.

(2 Tim. 1:7)

"For God hath not given us the spirit of fear; but of
power, and of love, and of a sound mind."
I have a sound and steadfast mind in Christ Jesus.

I have a sound mind, and I am heaven bound. And
in his words complete peace I have found.

(Gen. 18:14)

"Is anything too hard for the LORD? At the time appointed I will return unto thee, according to the time of life, and Sarah shall have a son." There is nothing too hard for the Lord because he holds my life card.

God can be seen everywhere—in your back yard, your barnyard, your church yard, your farm yard, and your courtyard because he is the keeper of every vineyard.

(Mal. 3:10-12)

"Bring ye all the tithes into the storehouse, that there may be meat in mine house, and prove me now herewith, saith the LORD of hosts, if I will not open you the windows of heaven, and pour you out a blessing, that there shall not be room enough to receive it. And I will rebuke the devourer for your sakes, and he shall not destroy the fruits of your ground; neither shall your vine cast her fruit before the time in the field, saith the LORD of hosts. And all nations shall call you blessed: for ye shall be a delightsome land, saith the LORD of hosts." Giving our tithes in the house of the Lord is called for in his word.

I have joy and excitement when giving my tithes
and offerings in the house of the Lord.

(Ps. 85:8)

"I will hear what God the LORD will speak: for he will speak peace unto his people, and to his saints: but let them not turn again to folly."
I will turn my ear to heaven to hear what the
Holy Spirit will say to me today.

The Holy Spirit's voice makes the enemy's voice disappear.

(1 Cor. 16:2)

"Upon the first day of the week let every one of you lay by him in store, as God hath prospered him, that there be no gatherings when I come." I am always willing to put my collection into the house of the Lord and receive divine connection.

Church collection does not need an election for we are his elect.

(Jer. 29:11)

"For I know the thoughts that I think toward you, saith the LORD, thoughts of peace, and not of evil, to give you an expected end." God is indeed our friend to the very end, and yes he will defend.

God does not have any evil thoughts toward us
because he has already overcome all evil.

(Ps. 61:1–3)

"Hear my cry, O God; attend unto my prayer. From the end of
the earth will I cry unto thee, when my heart is overwhelmed:
lead me to the rock that is higher than I. For thou hast been
a shelter for me, and a strong tower from the enemy."
God is our shelter in our stormy weather.

God is my shelter, protector, and the center of my life.

(Psalm 61:7–8)

God will preserve me and give me courage.

God will preserve and I won't let Satan get on my nerves
for God helps me overcome Satan's curveball.

(2 Tim. 2:15)

"Study to shew thyself approved unto God, a workman that
needeth not to be ashamed, rightly dividing the word of truth."
The advancement of the kingdom of God
requires the preeminent word of God.

To overcome the darkness, principalities, and powers of
this world, it is best to over study than understudy.

"I will abide in thy tabernacle for ever: I will
trust in the covert of thy wings. Selah."
I will safely hide under the wings of my King of Kings.

Under the wings of my King of Kings, I am provided all things.

(Job 42:2)

"I know that thou canst do everything, and that no
thought can be withholden from thee."
God will bless me with every good and perfect gift, and
I will continue to cling to the cross of Jesus Christ.

Jesus Christ is the root and offspring of King
David, and I am Abraham's seed.

(Eph. 6:16)

"Above all, taking the shield of faith, wherewith ye shall
be able to quench all the fiery darts of the wicked."
I will increase my faith and shut the gates of my enemies.

The saints are the conduit of faith that will move all our
mountains and give us victory time and time again.

(Romans 5:3–6)

The only hope for the ungodly is to believe in
the Lord Jesus Christ and be saved.

The ungodly cannot comprehend the sacred things of
God because they are indeed spiritually discerned.

(Num. 23:19)

"God is not a man, that he should lie; neither the son of
man, that he should repent: hath he said, and shall he not do
it? or hath he spoken, and shall he not make it good?"
God promised that he will make me to lie down
in green pastures; therefore, he cannot lie.

God is truth and his word is truth, and all things in the heavens
and the earth that were spoken by him are all truth.

(Rev. 21:22)

"And I saw no temple therein: for the Lord God
Almighty and the Lamb are the temple of it."
My body is the temple of the living God that makes me
the conduit of his anointing, power, and glory.

I am his honored vessel destined to fulfill all life's purposes.

"And I heard as it were the voice of a great multitude, and as the
voice of many waters, and as the voice of mighty thunderings,
saying, Alleluia: for the Lord God omnipotent reigneth."
The thundering voice of the Almighty God
will scatter the voice of the enemy.

The voice of God is mightier than the noise of
waters, thunder, rainfall, and earthquakes.

(Luke 6:39)

"And he spake a parable unto them, Can the blind lead
the blind? shall they not both fall into the ditch?"
If the blind lead the blind, both will become
confined and will not benefit humankind.

Being able to see is a gift from God, so cherish it
and help others to see the way more clearly.

(Mark 16:17–18)

"And these signs shall follow them that believe; In my name shall
they cast out devils; they shall speak with new tongues; They shall
take up serpents; and if they drink any deadly thing, it shall not hurt
them; they shall lay hands on the sick, and they shall recover."
Signs are promised as our spiritual guidelines
to manifest God's greatness.

God loves us so much that he will reveal all that Satan has undercover
and allow his saints to discover new dreams, visions, and revelations.

(Rom. 1:16)

"For I am not ashamed of the gospel of Christ: for it
is the power of God unto salvation to every one that
believeth; to the Jew first, and also to the Greek."
Satan will always put the blame on God, and God will
always be called the famous and fortunate.

I am not ashamed of the gospel of Jesus Christ for
I am claiming heaven as my paradise.

(Mark 12:17)

"And Jesus answering said unto them, Render to Caesar
the things that are Caesar's, and to God the things
that are God's. And they marvelled at him."
It takes a sincere, pure heart to compliment and
give to others what is truly due to them.

A sincere, pure heart will always rejoice at the good of others and
will make sure that the well-deserved compliments are given.

(Exo. 34:14)

"For thou shalt worship no other god: for the LORD,
whose name is Jealous, is a jealous God:"
Mark a jealous person; he or she will not compliment you sincerely
but seek more so to find out the cost of your precious things.

The countenance of a jealous person speaks value more than their words.

(2 Peter 2:1)

"But there were false prophets also among the people, even
as there shall be false teachers among you, who privily shall
bring in damnable heresies, even denying the Lord that bought
them, and bring upon themselves swift destruction."
Watch out for false prophets and false teachers. Most of the time,
they are full of themselves and will not attribute the true glory that
belongs to the everlasting God and Father of heaven and earth.

False prophets and false teachers are on earth to sharpen
Christians discernment in the supernatural realm.

(1 Kings 18:21)

"And Elijah came unto all the people, and said, How long halt ye
between two opinions? if the LORD be God, follow him: but if Baal,
then follow him. And the people answered him not a word."
There is a day coming when we will have to make a decision of
whose side we are on—whether God's or the devil's. I pray that
you will be bold enough to say, "I am on the Lord's side."

The side of the Lord is not divided because he is the
perfect one that abides forever and ever.

(John 4:23–25)

"But the hour cometh, and now is, when the true worshippers
shall worship the Father in spirit and in truth: for the Father
seeketh such to worship him. God is a Spirit: and they that
worship him must worship him in spirit and in truth. The
woman saith unto him, I know that Messias cometh, which is
called Christ: when he is come, he will tell us all things."
I will worship the Lord and ask for his mercies
that are given every morning.

When we worship the Lord, we release answers from heaven.

(2 Cor. 10:4)

"(For the weapons of our warfare are not carnal, but mighty
through God to the pulling down of strong holds;)"
My spiritual mind needs to be intact at all times
to differentiate the weapons of Satan.

When we are carnal, we are losing out on the release of the Holy
Spirit's power, the splendor of heaven, and everlasting life.

(Luke 10:19)

"Behold, I give unto you power to tread on serpents
and scorpions, and over all the power of the enemy:
and nothing shall by any means hurt you."
The saints of God will take communion together, break
bread, and unite in trampling the works of darkness.

God has given us his promised power to destroy
the works of Satan here on earth.

(Matt.11:28)

"Come unto me, all ye that labour and are
heavy laden, and I will give you rest."
If you are weary and troubled on every side, come to
Jesus just as you are, and you will find rest.

Your weariness will turn into blessedness.

(Mark 6:5)

"And he could there do no mighty work, save that he laid
his hands upon a few sick folk, and healed them."
Unbelief is a result of the rejection of the truth of who
God is; therefore, no one can truly say that he or she
loves God and does not believe in his word.

To love God is to believe that all his blessed promises
written in the inspired Bible are truth.

(Matt. 13:58)

"And he did not many mighty works there because of their unbelief."
The gift of healing is best manifested when one
believes in the power of the Holy Ghost.

When we believe the report of the Lord, we open
heaven to pour out blessings on earth.

(Matt. 9:35)

"And Jesus went about all the cities and villages, teaching in
their synagogues, and preaching the gospel of the kingdom, and
healing every sickness and every disease among the people."
More sickness and diseases will flee when the universal church
believes more firmly in the power of the Holy Ghost.

The Holy Ghost is ready to heal and deliver people
from the powers of darkness right here on earth.

(Mark.1:41)

"And Jesus, moved with compassion, put forth his hand, and
touched him, and saith unto him, I will; be thou clean."
Just a touch from the Lord makes all the difference
and changes one's life forever.

God's touch is so incredible and transforming
to the mind, soul, body, and spirit.

(Mal. 3:6)

"For I am the LORD, I change not; therefore
ye sons of Jacob are not consumed."
God is immutable, and all his promises made to us are
immutable. It is for us just to trust him and obey him.

I will exchange all my human plans for God's immutable plans.

(Phil. 4:19)

"But my God shall supply all your need according
to his riches in glory by Christ Jesus."
All my needs God will supply with his speed.

God is the all-time source of supplies that I need
each and every day, and he is always on time.

(Zeph. 3:17)

"The LORD thy God in the midst of thee is mighty; he
will save, he will rejoice over thee with joy; he will rest
in his love, he will joy over thee with singing."
When you come to God, heaven will sing and
rejoice with joy over your precious life.

God is able to do anything; he will sing, he will rejoice, he will
laugh, he will talk, he will dance, and the list goes on and on.

(Ps. 45:3)

"Gird thy sword upon thy thigh, O most mighty,
with thy glory and thy majesty."
We must have our spiritual sword of God ready to overcome
the flood and wicked devises of the evil one.

The word of God is our sword and must be sharpened
at all times to face Satan's onslaught.

(Ps. 62:11)

"God hath spoken once; twice have I heard this;
that power belongeth unto God."
The power of God empowers the believer to do greater
works and greater manifestation of the Holy Spirit.

The power of the most high God is needed in our daily lives so
that we will be able to withstand Satan in his troublesome hour.

(Ps. 93:4)

"The LORD on high is mightier than the noise of many
waters, yea, than the mighty waves of the sea."
Mightier than God you will not find, so stop your search
and start loving God and reading his words.

The power of God is so great that humans cannot even withstand
the earthly wind, much less the full power of God.

(Is. 26:4)

"Trust ye in the LORD for ever: for in the LORD
JEHOVAH is everlasting strength:"
God's strength has no length, and it is extended beyond our arm's length.

One day of God's strength on the human body can last for a lifetime.

The Lord's Prayer

"After this manner therefore pray ye: Our Father which art in heaven, Hallowed be thy name. Thy kingdom come, Thy will be done in earth, as it is in heaven. Give us this day our daily bread. And forgive us our debts, as we forgive our debtors. And lead us not into temptation, but deliver us from evil: For thine is the kingdom, and the power, and the glory, forever. Amen." (Matt 6:9–13)

About the Author

Rev. Dr. Sanneth Brown was born to proud parents Bishop Elijah Brown and Evangelist Estella Euphremia Brown in St. Mary, Jamaica, West Indies, as the last of fourteen children. As a Christian for twenty years, she is proud to carry the great mantle, bestowed upon her by her father, Prophet Elijah Brown, on August 10, 1994, the day before he died. God was and still is the center of the Brown family. After completing her nursing studies and training at Centennial College, Seneca College, and the University of Toronto, she became a full-time registered nurse for twenty-seven years with the PIECES Learning and Development Model of training qualifications, with a specialty in cardiac care, medical and geriatric nursing, Alzheimer's disease and Dementia.

After receiving her Bachelor of Religious education degree, being ordained as a reverend and a Certified Pastoral Counselor (CPC), she graduated with honors and received the Wesley White Award for her thesis titled "The Grace of God." She Obtained her Master of Theology degree with honors, and completed her doctorate degree in systematic theology (summa cum laude). She is now an ordained minister, a Christian clinical counselor, a Christian certified marriage counselor, and an ordained chaplain.

Her passion for souls and sincere desire to see people strive to be the best that God has designed them to be, motivated her to established a ministry called The New Testament Church of Christ the Redeemer of Canada. This is a focused prophetic church commissioned from God's Holy Throne: she speaks to nations, give clarity to those in authority, to declare and decree things yet to come, to intercede against all the plans of Satan, and to reveal the heart of a matter when it causes confusion to those in influential positions worldwide. Proverbs 29:18 says, "Where there is no vision, the people perish: but he that keepeth the law, happy is he." We must say only what God says, only what we hear from the throne of God. We believe in God the Father, God the Son, and God the Holy Ghost. This ministry is now seventeen years old. The church's mission is found in Luke 4:18–19, which says, "The Spirit of the Lord is upon me, because He hath anointed me to preach the gospel to the poor; he hath sent me to heal the broken-hearted, to preach deliverance to the captives, and recovering of sight to the blind, to set at liberty them that are bruised, to preach the acceptable year of the Lord." The church's motto is "Where thou goest I will be with thee."

Receiving awards such as, The Woman of Excellence award from the Glass Award Production, a Congratulatory letter in honor of her incredible leadership service in the community, presented by MP Shaun Chen, MP Dr. Raymond Cho, MP Rathika Sitsabaiesan, MP Neethan Shan, as well as other congratulatory letters from many members of parliament, councilors, and Canada's prime minister, Justin Trudeau, for her positive influence and tireless contributions to the community. She was also honored for her twenty years of hard work and outstanding leadership and was given an award in honor of Lincoln Alexander's legacy for Black History.

She is blessed with one son by the creator of heaven and earth, Darron Bailey Jr. He is the pride and joy of her life, her only God-blessed and prosperous child. He is spiritually ordained by the Holy Ghost to fulfill greatness in his destiny. He graduated from Ryerson University with a bachelor of psychology degree. Darron is the author of two books: his first is *Let There Be Laughs: Genesis and Exodus,* and his second is *Nine Plays for the Christians in All of Us.*

Dr. Brown enthrones Jesus Christ in her life. She reverences and honors God Almighty, her heavenly Father, and puts her entire trust in Him. Her future is secured in Christ Jesus because she is more than a conqueror through Christ that loved her (Rom. 8:37). She also believes in Matthew 28:19-20: "Go ye therefore, and teach all nations, baptizing them in the name of the Father, and of the Son, and of the Holy Ghost: Teaching them to observe all things whatsoever I have commanded you: and, lo, I am with you always, even unto the end of the world. Amen." She believes in Ephesians 6:19–20: "And for me, that utterance may be given unto me, that I may open my mouth boldly, to make known the mystery of the gospel, for which I am an ambassador in bonds: that therein I may speak boldly, as I ought to speak." Writing this book, is yet another piece to add to her divinely orchestrated achievements.

CPSIA information can be obtained
at www.ICGtesting.com
Printed in the USA
BVHW081411060519
547471BV00002B/35/P